MW00592480

dogs
up close

Vicki Croke

A Tiny Folio™

ABBEVILLE PRESS • PUBLISHERS

New York • London • Paris

contents

introduction

It's behind the beautiful blue eyes of the Siberian husky. Above the long legs of the Irish wolfhound. In front of the wagging tail of a golden retriever. Under the corded dreadlocks of the Komondor. Inside the chest of that big or little or thin or fat or shaggy or sleek or purebred or random-bred dog of yours.

It is love, loyalty, and more love.

For many, a relationship with a dog will outlast human relationships. We may bail out of a romance after a few months, but our love affair with dogs has prospered for more than ten thousand years. At one archeological dig in the Upper Jordan Valley in Israel, the remains of an elderly person clutching a young puppy were discovered in a burial site that was twelve thousand years old.

Dogs have been with us through the ages for good reason. You'll never hear from your dog, "You're a special person, but this just isn't working out for me." Or, "You think you had a rough day, wait till you hear about mine! The ball went under the couch and I couldn't get at it. The mailman came right through the gate and onto the porch. Again."

You will only get boundless and bounding joy for your mere presence: "You! You fabulous person! You're home, home at last with me!" There will be leaps and licks and squeals of joy. You will only get deep compassion for your pain or sorrow. "I'm right here, by your side," they say by placing a chin on our laps or a paw on our palms.

You will only get a non-judgmental friend who loves and admires you whether you received that promotion or not. Whether you're having a good day or a bad one. And even if you can't ever remember the punch line to a simple joke.

To your dog, you are you, wonderful you.

Throughout time, we've bred them for specific tasks: hunting, herding, guarding. They've kept our cupboards stocked, our sheep encircled, and our homes safe. But there's more. What all dogs give us are physical and emotional benefits that scientists are just beginning to measure and quantify.

One recent study at the State University of New York at Buffalo Medical School suggests that your dog will be of more comfort to you in a given stressful situation than your spouse. In this study, which gave people problems to solve or placed them in other anxiety-provoking situations, subjects were most stressed out with their spouses and most relaxed with their dogs. (A good reason to bring your dog, and not your partner to office parties.)

We know that dogs can be social bridges

for people who are withdrawn. And by distracting patients with their antics, dogs can help the seriously ill manage pain. Because we walk them, we are in better shape. Just caressing them lowers our blood pressure. And heart attack victims with pet dogs have a better one-year survival rate.

Our experts can not yet quite tell how or why this all happens. But you can keep the lab coats, just give me the labs (the black, chocolate, or yellow varieties).

As consistent as they are in their great hearts, they are glorious in their endless variety. There is tremendous choice, first in the hundreds of purebreds recognized worldwide and then the infinite variation in mutts or random-bred dogs. Whatever your taste, there is a dog for you.

The elegant Hungarian hunter, the viszla. The jowly, bustling Clumber spaniel. The perky Papillon. Tenacious terriers. Glamorous Afghans. Handsome German shepherds. Near-human

poodles. Those determined Nordics. The busting-out-all-over charm of goldens. The mind-over-matter toy breeds.

Can it be that after so many centuries of intimate contact our two species even look alike? We see Winston Churchill as a bulldog. Peter Lorre, a pug. And Meryl Streep, an Afghan.

But you don't have to search through history books to find doggie doppelgangers. Just walk down the street. We look for in a canine what we find aesthetically appealing, and often we think our own look quite attractive.

Sometimes, we seek in our pets the prettiness, power, or presence that we lack. The diminutive dandy walking the big great Dane. The plump lady with the svelte whippet. And the couch potato with the border collie.

They give us good health. A great attitude. A job well done. Love, comfort, and joy.

And what do we do for them? According to the statistics, more and more.

For one thing, it has been discovered that we can lower their blood pressure. We are feeding them better, or at least more expensively. And we are providing better and more advanced health care.

We sleep with them. Take them on vacation. Spend money on doggie shrinks ("Lassie, get help"). We talk to them. Play with them. And even take them shopping.

And when the horrible day comes that we must say good-bye to our faithful companions, we often send them out with the same rituals we would a family member. Of course.

For pets in the U.S., all of that loving adds up to $20 billion a year. And it's still the best bargain going. Even considering the stains on the rug. The pie swiped moments before company arrived.

The chewed Italian loafer. Those life spans that are just too brief.

We've come a long way since the pact was first struck by those unknown humans and long-forgotten wolves. But somehow, the same alchemy is at work today when a lonely widow feeds bonbons to her Pekingese. When a toddler tumbles onto the tummy of a patient mutt. When two stray dogs keep a lost boy with Down's syndrome warm through three cold nights in the Ozarks. When a big-hearted Newfoundland "saves" a swimming child.

When a stick is fetched. A tail is wagged.

When we look into the noble, knowing eyes of our beloved companions, and our hearts sing.

Asked the breed of her big black and white dog, one woman replied, "He's a nobody from nowhere." All of our dogs came from an unknowable and faraway land and time. The specific site

and second that this great bond began went unrecorded. You could say that all our dogs are nobodies from nowhere who have made us feel like somebodies from somewhere.

In **Dogs Up Close**, we celebrate the humor, kindness, courage, beauty, athleticism, heart, and soul of humanity's best friend.

dogs for all seasons

Dog owners never need step outside to witness climate change, for dogs bring the beauty of the ever-changing seasons in.

In spring, they track in mud; in summer, it is brambles and burrs; for fall, brilliant red, yellow, and orange leaves all over the carpet; and in winter—ah! winter!—it's snow balls stuck on dog legs and in between paw pads, later pools of water on the floor.

Of course, dogs not only bring the great outdoors indoors, they get us to go out. Studies have shown that dog owners tend to get out more than petless people do. That means they doggedly introduce us to winter, spring, summer, and fall. And though we must bundle up like Everest sherpas in winter and strip down to the bare minimum in summer, most dogs come fully equipped with all-weather gear.

The hair of the dog is a remarkably versatile garment. It is a terrific insulator against biting cold, and if kept well-combed and given plenty of loft, a dog's coat can also keep the animal cool in summer. Clearly, though, winter is preferred by the Newfoundland and summer by the whippet.

There are coats for all seasons. Naturally, Nordics and mountain dogs have dense, heavy coats, while breeds from Asia, North Africa, or India, have light, short coats. There are the corded, dreadlock coats of the little Puli and the huge Komondor—they can tolerate just about any weather conditions. Variety abounds: from the thick double coats of the Northern spitz type dogs such as Malamutes to the fine hair of greyhounds and pointers, from the hard, wiry coats of terriers to the non-shedding and fast-growing hair of poodles. Then, of course, there are those dogs such as the Chinese crested and the Mexican hairless with just about no coat at all.

How do those sled dogs of the North stay comfortable in that frozen world? The Finnish spitz has six hundred hairs per square centimeter—compare that to a dog like the little Yorkshire terrier with only one hundred hairs in that same space. Even the shortest-coated dog feels the exhilaration of the first snowfall, when their entire world changes. The smells are different, the temperature is different.

But we can imagine all of our dogs framed in the colors of every season, and always with that same eager expression, for every season brings new joy to our already happy pets. There's snow to tunnel through in cold weather. Water to swim in warm weather. In good weather there are more stinky things to roll in. In bad weather, there's messy mud to slog through.

A group of Shetland sheepdogs: blue merle,
tri-color, and sable included.

No matter the breed,
dogs like to take in the fall foliage—literally.

Old Bennington, Vermont,
a great place to get into the spirit of autumn.

An older dog enjoys the warmth
of the autumn sun.

A golden retriever reflected in the golden light of a pond.

A handsome golden retriever waits
near an antique vehicle.

A chocolate Lab pup investigates.

A shih-tzu in the doghouse.

Immersed in the wilds of Montana.

A child plays with a golden retriever. There is a natural understanding between dogs and children.

A golden retriever puppy among antiques.

A sporting dog in a domestic situation.

Pinschers as a breed began as ratters on German farms.

Murphy is a two-year-old cocker spaniel.

The Australian cattle dog is robust and fearless.

Jack Russells "share" a stick.

A young Irish wolfhound already displays nobility.

A low-slung, rugged hunter: the Basset hound.

Rocket, a German shorthaired pointer,
appears poised for take off.

A black Lab puppy among mallard decoys.

This English setter affects the air of
the country gentleman.

English springer spaniels are
gundogs with boundless energy.

A malamute has sweet dreams in the creamy snow drifts.

A hardy golden retriever pup enjoys the snow.

A young golden retriever catches
a scent and some sunlight.

Kirby, in the deep snow of Utah.

A handsome, rugged portrait of a canine and the cold of Colorado.

Pugsly takes whatever help he can get
to bear the elements in Utah.

Even the snow won't stop Sage from doing
his job—he's on point in Montana.

The good shepherd tends the snow.

Freeze frame: bounding through the drifts.

Surveying the frozen terrain from a rooftop.

Snuggling sled dogs.

The short undercoat of this Weimaraner
could use a bright overcoat.

Body heat: a husky and a dachshund sit tight.

A golden in snow.

So cold his whiskers are frozen.

No matter the size or breed, dogs love to cavort
together in the snow.

Our dogs will to follow us wherever we go,
even onto the ice.

The snow doesn't bother thick-coated
breeds of the North.

Nordics yawn in the face of cold.

Bearded collies can handle the winter.

The Bernese mountain dog is built to withstand the harshest conditions.

A Weimaraner takes in the warm rays.

This golden retriever enjoys the zinnias.

Golden retriever pup Cheddar inspects a log.

A beagle pup bounds through a field of flowers.

A chocolate Lab surrounded by purple
blooms in Arizona.

The beauty of a boxer set off by blossoms.

An English setter takes time to smell the flowers.

A German shorthaired pointer among the daffodils.

A chocolate Lab among yellow poppies.

Swimming in flowers.

A Shetland sheepdog in a forest of flowers.

The flower of the dog world:
the random-bred.

A warm nap in the great outdoors.

A golden retriever and a smiling Samoyed
take a break together.

Listening to nature.

German shorthaired pointer in a floral setting.

Best friends enjoy a soft meadow.

A golden retriever on golden sands.

The humor of an Irish setter.

Yellow
Lab,
blue
sky.

Getting to know you: close-up of a springer spaniel.

A day at the beach.

Sun, surf, and Spot.

An amphibious golden retriever.

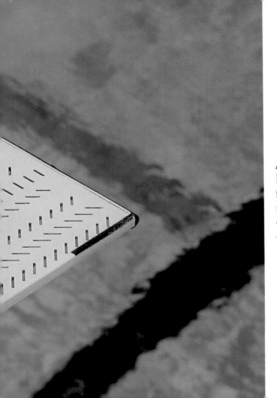

A Dalmatian finds the right spot on a hot day.

Bearded collies all in a row.

A fierce guard: Dogo Argentino.

Afghan hound in bloom.

A Komondor: the tough, corded protector
of the flocks in Hungary.

Bulldogs look skyward,
showing off a classic profile.

An American bulldog duo.

A happy Bouvier des Flandres. These dogs were bred
to guard, herd, and drive farm animals.

In the absence of sheep,
a border collie will herd anything.

Toy breeds are big in personality.

Sometimes small dogs feel a little crabby.

Floppy-eared bassets really know how to
get the low-down.

A pup with plenty of spunk.

Serious, gentle, and sensitive, the Bracco Italiano
is becoming popular again.

Vivid portrait of the sportsman:
the German shorthaired pointer.

the active dog

Graceful, powerful, energetic, athletic, tenacious, and tireless, the dog in action knows no bounds. From the long-limbed and lithe greyhound to the rock-hard mastiff to the magnificent mutt, canines are supreme athletes capable of dazzling us with their physical prowess.

Our dogs are built for action. Though they cannot see with the clarity of detail that we can, they have far better peripheral vision, the better to see the movement of prey. They can see some color, contrary to a popular misconception, and their nighttime vision is significantly better than ours. While we humans can hear up to twenty thousand cycles per second, our dogs can hear up to at least thirty-five thousand.

And then there's the nose. Dogs have two hundred million scent receptors compared to our paltry five million. It is estimated that their sense of smell is a million times more sensitive than our own. All of that adds up to important senses for the athlete.

Of course, the finely tuned eyes, ears, and nose are not always put to work in pursuit of live prey—or in pursuit of **anything** beyond some high-speed fun. As the photographs in this chapter attest, the active dog sometimes enjoys movement simply for its own sake. And if there is a body of water involved, so much the better.

Dogs on the go typically fall into two categories: the focused and the frenzied. The focused dog wears a look of intense concentration and operates with a definite goal in mind: to catch a flying frisbee, to leap a wooden rail, to ride the frothy surf (see page 123). Training is often necessary to achieve this level of focus, and not every dog is cut out for it.

On the other hand, just about every dog owner has witnessed the wide-eyed, tongue-wagging dash that signifies a canine gone temporarily loopy. From the owner's perspective it can look like a case of demon posssession, though here the demon is nothing more than a case of excess energy burning itself off. And who among us hasn't once wished we could run along with them, madly, our own tongues wagging in the breeze?

A golden retriever bounding for glory.

A water dog at full tilt.

An old English
sheepdog does laps.

Poetry in motion.

A Brittany on the run through a golden field.

A golden retriever dives into adventure.

Retrievers (black and yellow here) naturally love to retrieve things from the water.

The German shepherd is a skilled
and determined athlete.

Lassie hears "action" and obeys.

Never mind hang dog, witness the hang-gliding dog.

The big Kahuna.

A Lab takes a dive.

Chip shakes off the water: dogs usually like to do
this as close to their owners as possible.

This English springer spaniel shows off her agility.

A German shepherd takes the fast way down.

A terrier tussle: two wirehaired fox terriers.

Things get violent at a hound breeding farm.

A dog
making
waves.

Lift-off!

SD, likes long walks on the beach at sunset. . . .

working dogs

Some dogs may certainly be champion layabouts, but most are more than capable at pulling their own weight, and then some. They can chase down game and pull heavy sleds through deep snow. Dogs are unflagging sheep herders, mastering flocks with speed, agility, and calculated intimidation. Dogs can swim frigid lakes and muscle through thorny bushes. They can face down the terrifying tonnage of a bull or nimbly snatch a tennis ball from between two champagne flutes.

Many breeds perform one particular job particularly well. For example, greyhounds can reach speeds of up to forty-four miles per hour. Labs and pointers have webbed feet to power through the water. Sled dogs with their deep chests and well-muscled hind legs define the word endurance.

Our own pets can be found homing in on a frisbee with the focus and agility of a jet fighter. We have retrievers or mixes proudly straining to carry fifteen-pound branches along with them on a walk.

We have put our dogs to work for centuries. They hunted with royal parties in ancient China, India, Persia, and Egypt. Marco Polo reported seeing regal and rowdy packs of up to five thousand hounds out on a royal hunt in Asia. The Romans used fierce Mastiffs in gladiatorial combat. And they were employing the sleek grace of sighthounds in coursing events eighteen hundred years ago.

More recent efforts to measure and compare the athleticism of dogs have been underway for over a century. Ratting competitions for terriers began in the 1800s. And about one hundred years ago sled dog racing was initiated. There are field trials for sporting dogs and lure-coursing for sight-hounds. But all you have to do is throw a stick and you'll see an athlete at work.

Just like the wolf, dogs have semirigid hind legs and impressive thigh muscles, which provide power, endurance, and explosive energy. Flexible joints allow jumping (try as owners might not to allow it). And what they give up in limited rotation of the front legs, they gain in running stability.

With a well-muscled, powerful body; resilient and efficient heart and lungs; big teeth that can catch and hold and tear; a coordinated, smooth gait; joints built for graceful movement; plenty of brain power; plus excellent senses of smell, sight, and hearing, it is clear that the dog is a fantastically fit worker.

Dogs
ready for
the hunt.

139

Pack mentality.

Two labrador retrievers living up to their heritage.

A pointer looks back.

Brittanys strutting their stuff.

The pointer: elegant and focused.

Retrieving is the game: yellow Lab with a mallard.

Lead dogs turn the corner in a race
in Fairbanks, Alaska.

Lead dogs during a limited sprint race.

Steger's team pulls this sled over a pressure ridge
on the frozen Arctic Ocean.

The call of the wild.

Dog sled life at the South Pole. Dog teams have now been banned from the continent.

An Arctic Ocean run.

Sled dogs are the picture of determination.

Some dogs would rather take a ride.

A Komondor, one of the oldest breeds in Europe, with his flock. He is a tough guard, capable of protecting his charges against any predators.

A Komondor in action. Though clipped here,
the ropey coat of the breed protects the dog from
the harshest weather.

Regional sheepdog trials for the National Finals in
Dumfries, Scotland.

A Samoyed in training. This ancient breed is highly intelligent, eager for action, and undeniably beautiful.

Handsome, intelligent, alert, obedient:
the German shepherd.

A farm dog climbs the ladder of success.

The domestic dog's work is never done.

The true meaning of "love" from
a golden retriever puppy.

Dog gone fishing.

In shrimp boat heaven.

The Dalmatian has style but may be too spirited
and active for many owners.

Though Dalmatians were bred to run alongside trucks, sometimes a ride is preferred.

puppies

Fuzzy faces, button noses, round bellies, and stocky little legs. Is there anything cuter? Whether attacking a feisty blade of grass or snoozing on our laps, puppies are able to enchant even the most hard-hearted among us.

Though it may be difficult to get the hang of playing ball or learning how to go to the bathroom outdoors, our puppies get the sleeping thing down pat right away, mostly because growing is such hard work. During the first two weeks of a puppy's life, the young dog gains balance, sight, hearing, and even advances his sense of touch, taste, and smell.

From two to four weeks puppies begin to regulate their own temperature better, and, coincidentally or not, they wag their tails for the first time.

At four weeks, big things start happening: this is the socializing period. Let the games begin! Through hard, tumbling play, our pups will learn about dominance and submission as well as how to use their bodies to tackle, run, jump, sit, fall, chew, and maybe over the next few weeks, how to go to the bathroom outdoors.

This learning curve is as exhausting for puppies as it is for their owners. Our canine companions may know how to play hard, but thank goodness, they also know how to rest hard. And when puppies are asleep around us, everything is right with the world. Safe, peaceful, stress-free. The shared sense of peace is so deep it feels almost primitive.

In fact, for thousands of years dogs have acted as sentries for human camps. When they sensed danger, they alerted us. When they slept, it meant no harm was at hand. And though a Manhattan penthouse is far removed from the caves of Lascaux, and though the dog one is likely to find there—a Yorkie perhaps—is very different from the wolflike camp followers from so long ago, the dynamic remains the same. If our pups are calm, our souls get the signal to relax.

But it's not just the absence of danger. It's the presence of something wonderful, too. As Edith Wharton has expressed so succinctly, "My little dog—a heartbeat at my feet." Milan Kundara knows the same feeling. He has compared the sense of peace experienced while sitting next to a dog on a hillside to reentering Eden.

And when puppies are not relaxing, they are entertaining us with the almost cartoon-like versions of what they will do as adult dogs. Our little pups attack, herd, growl, bark, and chase . . . but clumsily and always endearingly.

A yellow Lab (a rambunctious breed)
pursuing an English pointer pup (a rather serious
and gentle breed).

You have a bright future in herding.

Casey, an English setter pup—a breed known
to be affectionate, loyal, and noble.

Trap, another English setter pup, displays
how handsome they are, too.

Portrait of Labs in black and white (yellow, actually). It's easy to see why these dogs are popular at home and in the field. Sensible, faithful, and athletic, they are the very definition of a dog.

177

A boxer showing off how cute she is
with uncropped ears.

It's not hard to see why golden retrievers also are so
popular. Loyal, loving, and absolutely gorgeous,
goldens make perfect companions.

Charming Chihuahua pup catches some rays.
This, the smallest of breeds, has a huge need
to be spoiled.

English setter pup catches a scent in the sunshine.

Even hardy nordic breeds enjoy some warmth.

Black Lab mother and pups. Because the breed is so popular and widespread, it is vital to find a good breeder to ensure one gets a healthy, stable pet.

Dalmatian pups peer over the edge
of their "whelping box."

Jana, a Rottweiler, waits quietly for company.

Sassy beginning to point.

A Chinese Shar-Pei pup: this ancient breed
is wrinkled even when young.

A mixed breed pup clearly has the best of everything.

Australian shepherd/blue healer pups are exhausted
just thinking about farm work.

Siberian husky pup, not yet pushing or mushing.

Sighthounds have eyes that look into your soul—
even when they're pups, as is this little lurcher (originally
greyhound/collie or greyhound/terrier crosses).

191

Dachshund pups: this is a lively and loyal dog that can become addictive for many people. Most owners not only stick with the breed, they tend to buy them in pairs.

With six you get Pekingese. . . . According to legend,
they are the offspring of a lion and a monkey.

Cocker spaniels with untraditional coloring. They are
shown in this country under three coat designations:
black, parti-color (patches of two or more colors), and
ASCOB (any solid color other than black).

Basset hound pups. Developed from the bloodhound, these low-riders are built to catch scents, but they are also gentle souls capable of oozing affection.

195

A Rottweiler pup, more fuzzy than fierce
at the moment.

Jack Russell terrier pups. Often called Jack Russell terrorists, these little creatures are full of spunk and spirit. They can be a challenge for owners.

The three faces of Labrador retrievers, all of them
sweet: yellow, black, and chocolate.

German shorthair pup up on point.

A wheelbarrow full of golden retriever puppies.

Lab pups at the doorway to adulthood.

Bedlington terrier pups: lamblike in appearance,
these little terriers possess the courage of lions.

Golden retriever pup—the ideal family companion.

Far from the coasts of Newfoundland and England,
where they were bred to retrieve, this black Lab puppy
plays with an apple.

Another black Lab puppy finds fun chewing straw.

Yellow Lab pups are introduced to a decoy.

This pointer pup is beginning to demonstrate its heritage.

Profile of a Shar-pei pup. The breed certainly has distinctive looks, with a head that is rather large in relation to its body.

English setter puppy on point.

A black Lab pup surrounded by ducks, sort of.

Jack Russell pups—always alert.

This pup shows off why Boston terriers
are so beloved. They are adorable little dogs
who live long and love well.

Even when lounging, pups look ready for action.

A Rottweiler puppy enjoys the great outdoors.
Rottweilers are intelligent—a little **too** smart
for many owners.

A springer who has already sprung and needs a nap.

An all-weather Lab
plays in the snow.

A Lab pup shows off his hardy heritage.

Pugnacious Jack Russell puppies hang on for ownership.

Two generations of elegance:
the Hungarian hunting dog, the Vizsla.

Irish setter pups strike a fetching pose. This is a dog is a great beauty and has a marvelous sense of humor.

rovers

There are more than four hundred breeds of dog around the world and despite names like Border collie and Border terrier, breeds don't respect borders at all. On a trip to Moscow years ago, I was amazed to see many collies. Aren't Russians supposed to have Borzois?, I thought. And how is it that poodles are so stylish at French cafes (when it is true they are not French at all, but probably German)? By this reasoning, a Scottish deerhound should be high-tailing it to the Highlands. And a Boston terrier should be pah-king the cah at Hah-vahd Yahd.

As we become global commuters, so, too, our best friends. We bring them with us to foreign posts because we can't bear to be without them.

Richard Byrd, for example, packed up his short-coated but beloved terrier Igloo with him on an expedition to Antarctica. He wasn't used as a musher but came purely as companion, and the little dog made it back with the explorer.

Igloo probably enjoyed the trip. Are there any travelers more enthusiastic than the dog? Just pick up the car keys and they are by our sides. "Ready!" they say with eager expressions and bodies coiled to spring out the door. There are few joys greater than a trip in the car. And these trips can even be expanded to include other forms of transportation. Granted, they cannot stick their heads out the windows of a Boeing 747, but still, the well-traveled dog is game to go.

Pull a suitcase down to pack and the dog is by your side. He or she looks into your eyes, "Am I going?" You keep folding and stowing. The dog keeps watching. When you reach the door, your new shadow is with you.

Ferries headed off the sandy beaches of Nantucket are usually packed with dogs. Transcontinental trains, vast oceanliners, and planes to all points have their share of canine cargo. The beautiful red-headed mutt I grew up with would sit under the elevated steps of our camper as we loaded our gear to ensure we would not forget her.

Dogs are sparkling jewels no matter the setting. We find dogs everywhere we find humans: in the cold north and the heated south, in skyscrapered cities and wide-open plains, amid mountains, flatlands, forests, and briny beaches. What we know is that to dogs—the most loving and loyal of all domesticated animals—home, hearth, and heart can be found wherever and whenever we are together.

All dogs love to stick their heads out of car windows.

A Labrador tail-gating party.

Though they may enjoy the breezes, dogs should
not ride loose in the back of a pickup.

A dog with a political agenda?

A Brittany's window on the world.

No matter where they go, good dogs make waves.

A Chesapeake Bay retriever needs to paint his wagon.

Tonya, in the striped desert of Utah.

A dog
with a view,
in Nepal.

Exotic love: A dog and cat in Indonesia.

On top of the world.

Cold comfort in Nepal.

A perfect setting for a golden dog in the Bahamas.

A West Highland white who is ready to go. These dogs are enchanting and assertive little characters.

Spotting a dog in San Juan, Puerto Rico.

A Swiss watchdog.

A sophisticated pooch in Alsace, France.

A bold Irish lass on the streets of Dingle.

Nepalese contentment.

A regal dog rests in Indian splendor.

Young, low, and urban.

A fawn Great Dane in fine form. This majestic animal was most probably bred to hunt wild boar.

248

The perfect setting for a German shepherd—
standing over the world.

A cocker spaniel enjoys the breeze in
Glacier Park, Montana.

To travel
with a
trusted
companion
is heaven.

Sunrise for sled
dogs in Alaska.

A pooch finds his place near Jericho in Israel.

Regal resting spot: the temple to Rameses III.

celebrities

Without a dog, a president is a little un-American.
A model simply pretty. And an actor, just one of
the pack. Dogs deliver more than affection, loyalty,
and courage. They can provide glamour, stature,
and, well, good breeding. Celebrities have known
this for years: dogs can lend warmth, status, or
stateliness, as circumstances require.

A terrier makes one seem more tenacious;
an Afghan hound imparts sophistication; a setter
suggests handsome wholesomeness. Dogs become
extensions of their owners and so become in a
sense one of the few personality traits one can
actually select.

The dog by our side tells the world something
about us. They provide a hint about personalities

and more than a clue about aesthetic judgments. What better choice for FDR than Falla? His Scottish terrier managed to symbolize both dignity and pluck for a country still reeling from the uncertainty brought on by the Depression. One of our most charismatic presidents—JFK—surrounded himself with dogs, owning at various times an Irish wolfhound, a spaniel, and a terrier.

A Great Dane lends substance to a sexy actress —matching grace with power. But there is a dog for every role. How do you play up Margaret O'Brien's sweet wholesomeness? Bring on the kind and courageous collie Lassie, of course. And since Lassie wouldn't be caught playing dead in a Manhattan watering hole, for Myrna Loy and William Powell a cocky, sharp little terrier named Asta is just the ticket.

And for artists and writers dogs can embody the notion of muse. It's not hard to imagine Eugene O'Neill's Dalmatian providing creative inspiration.

And even the non-celebrity knows a thing or two about image. Go to any dog show and head over to the toy dog ring—you'll find many of the plumper owners holding their petite charges. Look at your own pet and think about what you are telling the world: I'm pretty or spunky or powerful or athletic. (Or at least I want to be.)

We often laugh about our dogs living the good life, with nothing to do but enjoy our pampering. But they obviously have a huge job to do—they must complete our picture of ourselves. And over and over again, they prove they are up to the task.

So forget the facelift, the Ferrari, and the public relations firm. Just get a dog.

Frida Kahlo, the Mexican painter and wife of Diego Rivera, with a dog in 1944.

How surreal: Salvadore Dali and friend, July 8, 1949.

Eugene O'Neill looked upon his Dalmatian as his child,
even writing "The Last Will and Testament of
Silverdance Emblem O'Neill," which says, in part,
"No matter how deep my sleep I shall hear you,
and not all the power of death can keep my spirit from
wagging a grateful tail." This picture was taken in 1938.

Wearing an old skipper's cap, John Steinbeck leans against a tree during a stroll with Charley, the poodle of the best-selling "Travels with Charley," in 1962.

One of the most beloved presidents with one of the
most famous "first dogs": FDR and Falla, his Scottie.

Caroline's Welsh terrier, Charlie, makes a mad dash for the hospital at Otis Air Force Base on a visit to the First Lady, with JFK bringing up the rear in August 1963.

The Duke and Duchess of Windsor,
seen here with Trooper in 1953,
were absolutely devoted to their pugs.

A regal procession: Queen Elizabeth leads four of
the royal corgis at Liverpool Street Station in London,
January 1969.

Two cuties: Margaret O'Brien with Lassie.

The height of irreverence, wit, and sophistication:
Myrna Loy, Asta, and William Powell,
all of **The Thin Man** fame.

Rita Hayworth sings for a spaniel.

Spencer Tracy and—what else?—an Irish setter.

Two redheads: Joan Crawford and
a dachshund at home.

Jayne Mansfield with a Scottie and
a poodle ready to party.

What's black and white and red all over?
Glamorous Ava Gardner makes a fashion statement
with a Dalmatian.

Natalie Wood, Robert Wagner,
and a perky poodle.

The beautiful and dignified Grace Kelly with an
appropriately dignified breed, her Great Dane.

They must be popular with blondes: Kim Novak shows
off her Great Dane, Warlock, in 1960.

Audrey Hepburn with her dog from **The Nun's Story**.

Famed animal lover Brigitte Bardot with a dear friend.

President Reagan must wait for First Dog Lucky
to do what comes naturally after a long ride (even on
Air Force One), at Pt. Mugu Naval Air Station in
California, in 1985.

President Clinton with
the newest political pooch, Buddy.

selected bibliography

American Kennel Club. **The Complete Dog Book**. New York: Howell Book House, 1992.

Caras, Roger. **The Roger Caras Dog Book**. 3d ed. New York: M. Evans & Co., 1996.

Clark, Anne Rogers, and Andrew H. Brace. **The International Encyclopedia of Dogs**. New York: Howell Book House, 1995.

Fogle, Bruce. **The Encyclopedia of the Dog**. New York: Dorling Kindersley, 1995.

Kilcommons, Brian, with Sarah Wilson. **Good Owners, Great Dogs**. New York: Warner Books, 1992.

Serpell, James, ed. **The Domestic Dog: Its Evolution, Behavior, and Interactions with People**. New York: Cambridge University Press, 1995.

photography credits

Editor: Jeffrey Golick
Designer: Jordana Abrams
Picture Editors: Naomi Ben-Shahar and Scott Hall
Production Manager: Vicki Russell

First edition
10 9 8 7 6 5 4 3 2

Cataloging-in-Publication Data
Library of Congress
Croke, Vicki.
    Dogs up close / by Vicki Croke. — 1st ed.
        p.   cm.
    "A tiny folio."
    Includes bibliographical references
(p.   ).
    ISBN 0-7892-0428-2
    1. Dogs.   I. Title.
SF426.C76   1998
636.7—dc21   97-43082

selected list of tiny folios™ from abbeville press

- angels • 0-7892-0403-7 • $11.95

- ansel adams: the national park service photographs
  1-55859-817-0 • $11.95

- art of rock: posters from presley to punk
  1-55859-606-2 • $11.95

- barbie: in fashion • 0-7892-0404-5 • $11.95

- elvis: his life in pictures • 0-7892-0157-7 • $11.95

- the great book of french impressionism
  0-7892-0405-3 • $11.95

- hot rods and cool customs • 0-7892-0026-0 • $11.95

- the life of christ • 0-7892-0144-5 • $11.95

- minerals and gems from the american museum
  of natural history • 1-55859-273-3 • $11.95

- norman rockwell: 332 magazine covers
  1-55859-224-5 • $11.95

- treasures of folk art: the museum of
  american folk art • 0-7892-0409-6 • $11.95

- treasures of the louvre • 0-7892-0406-1 • $11.95

- wild flowers of america • 1-55859-564-3 • $11.95